A Battle For More

Chanda Ford

CHANDA FORD

ISBN: 0-578-46961-8
ISBN-13: 978-0-578-46961-4

DEDICATION

To the people that are going through their own battle for more and need a reminder that you are not alone.

CHANDA FORD

CONTENTS

In and out of relationships.

Settling. Hurt. Depressed. Searching.

There has to be more...

ACKNOWLEDGMENTS

To each person that played a role in the journey to loving me. You fought for my life when I didn't have the courage to fight for my own. You saw me when I felt invisible. You heard me when I didn't know the words to say.

Thank you all for everything.

"Maybe the journey isn't so much about becoming anything. Maybe it's about un-becoming everything that isn't really you so you can be who you were meant to be in the first place." – Author Unknown

A Battle For More

CHANDA FORD

1 THE TURNING POINT

It was the year of 2013 when I first heard what I know now to be God.

I was depressed.

I was in a relationship that went a year and three months longer than it should have. I gained forty-five pounds. I was secluded from friends. I had a face of happiness everywhere I went. It was while in this relationship my want for something deeper grew more. I was in a state where I was desperate for change. It was in this low period of my life that I listened for the voice of God.

Around this same year, my Pastor started a series on taboo subjects; marriage, sex, etc. He taught about living a life for God and obeying His word. I have heard similar sermons before, but this time was different. This time I conviction came upon me about my lifestyle both current and past. Moving in and out of relationships in hope that the next will be my last and forever. Believing the next will fill the voided space longing to be filled. Acting as though I was the wife when I was barely treated as a girlfriend. I was tired of living life my way.

I was in a relationship that had a pleasant start (as they all do) and a rocky middle. He wooed me with dates and spending time which was something that I was missing in past relationships. Kind gestures had me in awe of someone that I barely knew. About four months into the relationship, I witnessed a drunken, jealous rage that I had never seen or experienced before. He stumbled through the door yelling about being told of a previous relationship and my working relationship with the males in the office where I worked. I called a friend of his while running every possible scenario through my mind preparing for what may come next. With no answer from his friend, I was thankful he went to sleep after an hour or so of angry ranting. He didn't remember the previous night's activity even after informing him of the cursing and accusations made. Of course, at this moment, he had to go, right? That's how I felt then, but it's not what happened. He remained.

Opposition isn't always from an enemy. He didn't come in the house drunk again, but there were other major disagreements which occurred about trust and friends, specifically mine. A few arguments resulted in me leaving the house. One night in particular, he called my parents as he began gathering his belongings. They were unaware of any previous altercations fueled by jealousy and distrust. My parents were in the house talking with him when I pulled in the driveway. One parent remained in the house while the other came out to the car to discuss why he was packing. Upset, crying and attempting to share everything up to this moment, I was met with a response that I was not expecting. It was a response of sympathy towards his situation. It was a response of how communication may be the issue and to consider allowing him to stay at least until he can find somewhere to live. Listening to the pleading and willingness to do all they can they can to "make things better" including pointing out scripture, I felt defeated! I felt my feelings didn't matter. I didn't matter!

I gave up!

He and I began attending church, Bible Study and Sunday School together. On the surface, we had a fresh start and was working out. He sought advice from others including family in hopes to improve the relationship. We began working on our communication and getting to know one another. Everything appeared to improve until another argument erupted. I was home for several weeks after surgery at this time. While he was at work, a couple of coworkers came to the house to check on me and bring a gift from the office. The issue wasn't about them bringing a get-well gift. The argument was about one of them being male and coming to the house while he was not there. We went back and forth as I explained the male coworker was not alone but with a female. Then, something hit me! I had surgery a few weeks ago and was arguing about who came to my house to bring me a gift.

Change doesn't come easy!

Depressed and crying in secret, I was weary in trying at this relationship. There was a battle on the inside and one on the outside. I had a fight about leaving and one about staying. It was like a game of tug of war. I knew my situation was not healthy. I yearned for something different, something real. Obstacle after obstacle, I had reached a point of surrender but not to people. I wanted to see what living for God was about. I remember sitting in a parking lot crying and ready to walk away from it all; family, my house, my job, everything just to live. I recall speaking to a friend about this feeling warring within me. She didn't encourage me to leave. She encouraged me to fight for the life God has for me. I didn't fully understand what she meant at that time, but I began to believe what she said also it had to be better than what I was experiencing.

It's hard fighting the public's opinion.

For months, he was trying to stay. I was ready to leave. I wanted to just be free. He went to church members for advice even arranged a meeting to my surprise. The married couple came ready to counsel us through a rough patch only to be informed I was unaware of why we were meeting. They were asked to be mediators in our relationship while I was told that we were going for lunch after church. In a public place before strangers, I fought to hold back the tears of hurt, anger, embarrassment and mostly being vulnerable. They were all emotions I battled to not reveal to the public most my life up to that point. Battles seen and known only by few.

The battle definitely was not mine!

I didn't understand at the time, there was another battle. One unseen and unknown to me. I didn't realize how my life had gone from living to barely existing. I conformed every area of my life including work. Satisfying the jealous, abandonment feelings of his and carrying the weight of the opinions expressed by others. Everything was so subtle. An occasional girls night out with friends was no longer an option, so we can do things together. My alone visits to see my parents were few and brief because he stopped by to see if they needed him to do anything. To the public, we were a happy couple spending time together. In reality, I had given up the battle for living my life. I thank God for praying friends. They were unaware of the details, but they recognized something greater going on. They were in constant prayer fighting for my life! I knew unhappiness had taken over but didn't realize how withdrawn I had become. Later, several friends shared how they felt a loss of their friend and anger toward what was going on.

Your way of leaving or dealing with a situation will not look like God's way.

One morning after Sunday school, we had a few minutes before church. I was sitting at the end of the last row irritated after another disagreement that morning. While waiting, I distinctly heard a voice say, "Let go." When I turned around, no one was standing behind me or on the side of me. I was puzzled. What was that, and what did it mean to "let go?" I pondered over those words for the rest of that day. In addition to the emotional stress, there was a loan we shared that needed to be dissolved, and I had my way of getting it done. I composed a letter of agreement stating the breakdown of how things were to be divided and repaid. I was even prepared to get it notarized. The only thing on my mind was to not be the only one left holding the baggage of debt.

The situation defeating you may actually be the one strengthening you.

I struggled with the payment arrangement designed to recoup at least half the remaining debt of the loan. At this time, we had agreed to part ways and be friends. He didn't fight the financial split and was willing to sign the typed document plus gave me some money towards the debt. I had no peace with the decision of this agreement. Imagine how I felt when peace came from me tearing up the agreement and considering the payment as debt paid in full. I learned in God's word that all things work together for good when we love Him. I was struggling with my identity when asked to be vulnerable before strangers. I was struggling with knowing God when His word was being used to keep me in bondage and free me at the same time. At a time that I was struggling with why things were happening, I had to do what comes hard for most people. This is where my journey for more really began. I had to let go.

So I did.

2 INTRODUCTION

I'm unsure of the exact moment. I recall talking to my roommate about something missing, wanting more and just being tired. Filling voids or pains with alcohol or cigars was no longer an option. Doing church as usual was not the answer. Something changed. Briefly, we visited other churches together only to look at each other later and agree that was not the place. My search eventually led me to stay home and watch various ministries on television. Something awakened in me. And I found, He was there the entire time.

"For I know the plans I have for you," declares the Lord, "plans to prosper you and not to harm you, plans to give you hope and a future. Then you will call on me and come and pray to me and I will listen to you. You will seek me and find me when you seek me with all your heart." Jeremiah 29: 11-13 (NIV)

When I began writing this, I had no idea that it was going to turn into the start of something much bigger than me. I didn't understand why I was typing it and being a book was the farthest from my mind. Most of what's on these pages came from my journaling about my past and some of my day to day struggles. It wasn't until a couple of people read it that I began to wonder if it's more to this. I must be honest and say discouragement came upon me a few times. There was even a moment when I stopped writing. To be honest, outside of my personal story, there isn't anything new. Everything that I'm saying has been said before in one form or another. So, if that's the case, who is this for? Was I only writing this for the couple of people that liked it and myself? It's interesting how one word or question can take life or speak life. After months of no writing or even thinking about these pages, I was asked where's the rest of the book.

The rest?

Maybe there's more to these pages. If so, who is this for? Maybe it's for a young adult in an unhealthy relationship and think they must stay. Maybe it's for someone that needs to know they are not the only one wondering about life. Maybe this is just another test being used for me to step out of my comfort zone. Maybe God wanted me to just show the simplicity of living a life with Him and for Him. And to let someone know that no matter how hard things may seem, He was still there. He's still here now. There's purpose behind all the battles. We only need to keep trusting Him and the process He's taking us through.

I'm far from a bible scholar. I am a young lady who decided to start putting her thoughts on paper while seeking to know God. For years, I have taken the struggles of my life and put them on replay. I continuously remind myself of what was, settling for whatever, and afraid of what could be.

The events that I shared above was not to knock any of the people involved. Months after the relationship, I understood that those events happened for a reason and was part of God's purpose. We met in the middle of our process. Two people needing to learn who we were individually. Existing in life while carrying around the pains of our past and expecting a new relationship to be the answer to it all.

> *"For I'm going to do a brand-new thing. See, I have already begun! Don't you see it? I will make a road through the wilderness of the world for my people to go home, and create rivers for them in the desert!" Isaiah 43:19 (TLB)*

One of my main interests prior to this was helping people to get into shape with cleaner eating habits and exercise, so I thought about creating a guide, something different. I started reading books on weight loss, eating, and even considered certifications. In my mind, people will not listen if I didn't look a certain way. After all, that's what we see on TV and in magazines. We see lean, toned individuals helping others get into shape. Therefore, there was a delay in my journey, because I wasn't there yet. I was coaching others by using the information that I had learned, but I didn't feel qualified to do what was in my heart. I needed to focus more on practicing what I was preaching or so I thought.

During that time, I began sensing a nudge within. Close friends were asking when I was going to start doing this as a business or something. Strangers began talking to me from what seemed out of nowhere. Why me, was a question that I began asking often. I wasn't ready or qualified by society standards. I still had work to do. Truth is, I thought it was just my outer appearance that needed work, but there was much more.

Have you ever experienced something on the inside tapping at you and then pushing you like a sense of urgency? If so, what did you do?

Well, I got stuck. Stuck in fear and excuses of not being enough, not having enough, and not doing enough. I sensed pressure of being who everyone else said I was and doing what everyone else wanted. This place was not unfamiliar to me. I've been here on several occasions in life. Almost every time an opportunity to move came, I got stuck with what seemed no one to turn to for assistance or encouragement. What made this time different from any other, there were people strategically placed in my life to speak something different and reminded me to ask...

What did God want?

Months after letting go of the relationship, I was hungrier than ever to know more. I began to have a sequence of conversations about having a relationship with God, recognizing His voice and learning to obey Him. I started to recognize a connection between our relationship with God to our overall health. The role our understanding of God plays in where we've been, where we are and where we are going.

Relationship. Health. Purpose.

Knowing God and His role in our life is a process, and God took me on a journey of discovery of them both.

After ending yet another unsuccessful relationship, it was time to take a break. *A long break.* Now, this was easier said than done. There were a couple of male friends to enter the picture during this time. They were short lived and proved to be distractions. Obstacles placed on the road to hinder my journey to Him.

I placed myself on a timeout for doing life as usual and just settling for whatever and whoever crossed my path. It was time to get serious about my relationship with God, my health and seeking my purpose. I needed to step away from all distractions. I decided to date God, myself and seek real change in my life.

Being healthy is about more than how much you weigh or the size clothes you wear. No longer just looking the part but to walk the part. *Webster defines health as the condition of being sound in body, mind, or spirit.* Healthy is showing physical, mental or emotional well-being.

Condition and appearance.

I guess that's why people assume smaller individuals are healthy. You can't judge a book by its cover. In my opinion, both definitions should read "and" instead of "or" because you can't achieve true balanced health without any of the three working together. They are connected. That's like getting new tires and washing your car but not having gas or the oil changed. Your car will look good, but the neglect to the operating system will prevent it from traveling at a distance.

3 FRESH START

We start every year with a get healthy campaign. The commercials encourage us to lose weight, buy new clothes, try a new adventure, etc. The planning begins in November at the start of the holiday meal plans. December, we begin setting money to the side for our fresh start come January. We celebrate the coming of a new year with our resolution in mind and start date set for Monday. Maybe a month into the year, something comes up. The resolution comes to an end. Then, we spend the rest of the year feeling like we failed and unable to move forward.

We hold on to every memory of missing the mark and every negative comment spoken mentally also verbally. Now, we have another year spent on reflecting on what didn't happen that year and those past. We become stuck in reliving our past failures rarely acknowledging any successes. Have you ever thought of the fact that we can't move past the perceived failures because we are hoarders? *A hoarder is defined as one who accumulate for preservation or future use in a hidden place.* What things or people are you hoarding but need to let go?

We are good at holding on to things that we think may become useful again like clothes. A woman, for example, will keep a closet full of clothes she can no longer wear. If she gains weight, she will shop for new clothes to wear, but she doesn't remove the old ones from her closet. She pushes the old clothes to the back of the closet for that day she can wear those garments again.

Hoarding.

We do the same with relationships of our past. What about those numbers kept in our phone or the black book in the dresser? You know the book in your sock drawer in the back-corner tucked underneath everything for a rainy day. What about those "friends" placed in a glass case that says, "break in case of emergency"? You know those "friends" you call when you're lonely or upset. What about the memories that you hold on to for times when you're feeling like you're not worth better? The people telling you that you can't and won't ever be able to do all you set out to do.

Why do we not hoard the Word of God instead? We learn

that He's more than enough. He is our comforter when we are lonely. He is our healer when we are hurt. We learn that He is always there when we need Him. The word reminds us that He loves us so much that He gave His Son to die for our sins. Now, that's worth remembering. Could it be that we don't or are unable to hoard these words because its been made too complicated? Maybe, we are questioning who He is because most information outlets are jumbled with static. Or maybe, it has been hard to see Him in your life due to the clutter.

A new start should begin by removing some things. We need to learn who we are and how to love that person no matter where they are. We don't have to wait for a new year or a Monday to have the fresh start for more. What if we start now with clearing the clutter as we search for more?

Let's do some cleaning up!

4 SEARCHING FOR MORE

God's love for us started before the womb setting the foundation for the rest of our life, but our upbringing and environment can shake or shift some things. Some grow up with a loving dad and mom in the household that may guide them through life, talk to them about God, and provide support. Does it mean they won't experience some negativity, get sidetracked, be heartbroken, become a young parent, or any other lifestyle change? No. There are things that we are going to do and go through regardless of our upbringing.

My parents were both active in my life; mostly my mom. My dad worked out of town often. When he was home, he rested. My parents loved me, but it didn't prevent me from experiencing some rough patches. At the age of five, I wanted and tried to take my life unknowing to them even at the time of me writing this. I experienced some bullying in my adolescent years around the neighborhood and at school.

With my siblings out of the house or almost out, my pain needed a place to go, so it went towards my parents while living under their roof. Those early years, I clung to my mother and avoided my father. As I got older and right before moving out, I secluded myself more by staying out late or not coming home at all. Anger, frustration and self-hatred was building inside.

I saw and experienced my share of abuse and heard plenty of negative language. My relationship foundation was shifted. Here's the thing about a foundation, you can cover it up with nice flooring or concrete, but after a while, the cracks will begin to show up somewhere. The first cracks were covered with a smile. On the rainy days, the smile needed a little help, so a little hidden bottle of alcohol patched those weak areas. Later, the little dose of alcohol turned into much more than a little. I needed to maintain a decent appearance and reputation, so I didn't overindulge to cause any alarms in that area.

But alarms should have been raised in other areas. I rebelled against my mom, stopped going to class and partied all of the time. It impaired my decisions when talking to guys, and I began accepting whatever form of relationship they had to offer which wasn't much. My adult years of dating was spent mostly trying to avoid being hurt by not opening up much and giving a very short leash on what I will tolerate. Though, it didn't stop much. I was still heartbroken. I questioned being good enough or worthy of anything good. I was a loner for the most part that accepted relationships with no regard of the damage it may cause me physically or mentally.

This was basically the cycle that I had over and over again. Did I know better? Yes, but I didn't expect better for me. Then, came that first nudge of more. The more that I needed all the while!

God!

"In the beginning, God created..." Genesis 1:1

It is amazing the path this battle for more has taken my life over the years and various seasons to get to where I am now. As a very young child, I can remember not wanting to be in the home that I was raised in or continue life. I remember on a couple of occasions lying in bed crying, wondering what I can do to leave. Once as a child, I wrote a letter to my mom, placed it in her dress pocket as I planned to run away. With my little red suitcase packed, I didn't make it any further than hiding in the back of a closet. I had a knife that I stashed away in a box where I kept a lot of miscellaneous items. One day, thoughts of words spoken from other kids, how I looked, and events witnessed at home ran rapid through my mind.

I took out the pocket knife and ran it as hard as I could across my wrist only to find welts left on my skin.

Why did the knife cut everything else except me?

At twenty-three, I was in a car accident that by the opinion of some should have seriously injured me if not killed me. Riding home with a friend in a small four-door car, we were hit on the passenger side by a large extended cab truck. It was like everything was in slow motion. I saw the truck as it ran the blinking red light and hit my door. Glass shattered as I turned my head, and the car went around approximately three times stopping just before going into the brick wall of the hospital. I recall being extremely calm as the ambulance, police cars, and fire trucks came on the scene. Answering all the questions of the man sitting in the backseat with what seemed to be a sheet covering me, the firemen cut open the door of the car. I walked away with only a two inch deep wound on the back of my shoulder from the metal frame of the car seat. The nurse called me lucky. My dad called me blessed.

My thought, why did I survive?

To be honest, it was not until my thirties that this burning for more grew beyond settling for life and turned into a search for purpose. I began a quest for more. A pursuit for God. A search for understanding. An answer to my question of why I was even here. I didn't know where this search was going to take me, but I felt ready. There had to be more to life or at least a reason for the roads I was traveling. Have you ever felt like that?

"Are you tired? Worn out? Burned out on religion? Come to me. Get away with me and you'll recover your life. I'll show you how to take a real rest. Walk with me and work with me-watch how I do it. Learn the unforced rhythms of grace. I won't lay anything heavy or ill-fitting on you. Keep company with me and you'll learn to live freely and lightly." Matthew 11:28-30 (MSG)

Like most people, I have attended church for most of my life. To know God or be close to Him seemed rather confusing. I suppose that's a good word for it. Listening to the ones around, He wasn't someone or something that you can know personally. You had to be special or someone in high authority to even talk to Him, and I was not going to tell someone outside of myself the things on my mind.

Around the age of six, I had this thought or image. I pictured God as someone sitting high in the sky on a cloud looking down at us. Every person had strings tied to every joint of their body, and God was the puppet master (one who makes and entertains with puppets). I thought that God was controlling every move people made. How could I minimize Him to something I've seen on TV? I felt so silly for having such a thought, so I never shared it with anyone. As comically as that sounds though, I suppose I wasn't too far off the mark for a six-year-old. He's not a puppet master in the sense of the definition, but He is in control of everything.

"Remember the things I have done in the past. For I alone am God! I am God, and there is none like me. Only I can tell you the future before it even happens. Everything I plan will come to pass, for I do whatever I wish." Isaiah 46:9-10 (NLT)

God is in total control. He knows what happened, what is happening, and what will happen. His plans do not change based on current events. Absolutely nothing happens without His permission. Satan may prowl and seek to destroy but even he must ask for permission before doing anything. Satan cannot touch a hair on your head without permission from God. Satan is not equal to God for he too was created by God.

God knows all things, but it should not stop you from

talking to Him about any and everything in your life. It's called having a relationship. And yes, you can talk to Him. No matter who you are or what you have done. Day or night. In the car, at work, or sitting on the couch. It is not required for you to go through any person to speak with God only Jesus. If you listen, you'll find that He is and has been talking to you too.

I made a conscious decision to stop the cycle with me. It's not about the events themselves that occurred in the past but more about what God wants to do with it. I no longer want to allow them to control my life any further. I want my life to be about having a relationship with God and learning love through Him instead of a lack of concern due to painful memories of the past.

5 SEARCHING FOR RELATIONSHIP

Cambridge Dictionary's meaning of relationship is the way two or more people are connected, or the way they behave toward each other. I didn't understand why most of my relationship seemed to begin and end the same. The search for more led to a look into how relationships are created in the beginning and the affects each have on the next. Before we enter the world, we are introduced to relationships.

"Thus says the Lord, your Redeemer, and He who formed you from the womb..." Isaiah 44:24 (AMP)

The womb of a woman sets the groundwork for the relationships to come. It's the place of love and nourishment. In the womb, a baby hears the voice of its mother, father or other people that will be a part of their life. A baby does not care what the people look like during the incubation stage. All the baby knows is their voice of peace, who cares, and who to possibly trust. They detect those that may cause harm or cannot be trusted all by the sound of their voice. It stems from the vibrations and sounds while in the womb. Have you ever noticed the reaction of a baby to the person that yelled while they were in the womb? The baby, after birth, hears their voice and may cry. Or if being held by that person, they may squirm to be free. A relationship has been formed whether positive or negative all by the sound of a voice.

A burning for more

Just as your relationship with loved ones began in the womb, your relationship with God began there when He spoke and created you. To be honest, His relationship with you began before the womb.

"You made all the delicate, inner parts of my body and knit me together in my mother's womb. Thank you for making me so wonderfully complex! Your workmanship is marvelous-how well I know it. You watched me as I was being formed in utter seclusion, as I was woven together in the dark of the womb. You saw me before I was born. Every day of my life was recorded in your book. Every moment was laid out before a single day had passed." Psalm 139:13-16 (NLT)

God knew the when, where and why of your creation. Think about that for a minute. Before any signs were given to your mother, God knew. So, you were not a mistake. You didn't just happen. You may have been a surprise to them, but not to the One that took the time to make sure every part of you was placed just the way He wanted. He has a purpose for you!

"Then God saw everything that He had made, and indeed it was very good..." Genesis 1:31 (NKJV)

An understanding of more

As you get older and events happen in your life, your

search for a relationship with God may change. You may begin to question His voice, His existence, and His love. You may get angry and discouraged at the outcome of events. But guess what? His relationship with you does not waver. You see His way is nothing like ours. With us, relationships come and go. We would stop speaking with someone for something as simple as them not doing what we want. What if God stopped loving us because we wouldn't do what He wants? He would have left us alone at a very early age. We wouldn't even be having this conversation. And because He knew all this, He sent His Son for our salvation, and the Holy Spirit as our Helper. God is the Father, the Son and the Holy Spirit referred to by some as the Trinity! One God in three Persons serving different tasks and loving us the same. As you continue to seek an understanding of more, it helps to know Him to build a relationship.

I must explain it the way that I understand now because this was part of my confusion mentioned earlier as well. I didn't get the whole relationship with God. It was hard for me to connect to someone when I had no clue as to who He was. I heard all these different names, told to read the Bible for myself, pray to God for wisdom, pray in Jesus name, and Jesus died for you. I read parts of the Bible. I was unsure about praying all together. I went to Vacation Bible School, Sunday school and participated in the Holiday programs. Yet, I still had no clue. Churches, at least the ones I attended, spoke of God and Jesus as two totally different people, and well the Holy Spirit was something mentioned rarely if at all. I wasn't too sure about the role the Holy Spirit played in all this. Let me just say, it was a relief to find they are the same God and not two or three different gods. Oh, and the Holy Spirit was like my conscience guiding me but much better. There's a little more to it all and many can go deeper, but my purpose here is to keep it simple. I'm still learning as I continue to desire more of an understanding (as this is a daily walk), but this was the basic introduction that I received which helped me.

6 IMAGINING MORE

For years, I have had an issue with the image looking back at me in the mirror. I have been on just about every weight loss program you can think of plus the occasional exercise videos. Each to only last but a season. My image complex did not stop at my weight. It extended to being mentally consumed with other people's opinions of me. I was trying to be who they thought I should be. Whether I should further my education or not. They were ignoring my feeling of not being enough, not important enough and the feeling of failure because I missed the mark of expectations. This is not to say that I didn't accomplish anything. But, was it enough?

As women, we are known to tear apart the reflection looking back at us. Flabby stomach with rolls all around. Big thighs. Skin, hair and even feet. We are our own worst critics when it comes to acceptance even beyond the physical. What is the real issue?

"Then God said, "Let Us (Father, Son, Holy Spirit) make man in Our image, according to Our likeness [not physical, but a spiritual personality and moral likeness]; ...So God created mankind in his own image, in the image of God he created them; male and female he created them." Genesis 1:26-27 (AMP)

Acceptance of more

This seems to be a good place to start. God's image.

Acceptance of our image as men and women has been based on man and media from birth. The images flashed on TV screens and in magazines are of "perfection". Man's idea of perfection. Males have the chiseled abs, rippled arms, toned legs and every string of haircut and placed just right. Ladies are slim with not even a pudge, no cellulite to be seen, and hair full of body. Perfect, right? Even now, we label babies as fat, ugly, and bad before they begin walking or talking. Making imaging more to be difficult with every negative thought and image spoken into their life before they know what their physical image is. Rarely are there words of life and positivity. Healthy, beautiful, good…just to name a few.

I am not sure about as a baby, but negative names were spoken to me when I was an adolescent. Sometimes, it still occurs. I vividly recall loved ones calling me names like "big draws" in front of others. Telling me things like "you're pretty but you would look so much better if….". Schoolmates and neighborhood kids speaking harsh words due to my skin, family or even threats to cut my hair. Being judged and picked on for things that I had no control of. Attempting to act as if I'm unbothered while at the same time wondering if it's true. How many of you have experienced similar accounts? How many of you are doing the same to your kids, family members, or friends?

Imaging more

We are created in the image of God. Most of us have heard this for years. I decided to do a little searching. Image, in Merriam Webster, has several meanings. Here's a couple: a reproduction or imitation of the form of a person or thing; a visual representation of something. When we normally use the word image, we think of something physical that can be touched or seen. But here's the thing, God's image is not physical. God is spirit. God is not physically seen until part of the Trinity of God became flesh, Jesus (God the Son, the Word). So, this led me to search for the physical image of Jesus.

"...One like the Son of Man, clothed with a garment down to the feet and girded about the chest with a golden band. His head and hair were white like wool, as white as snow, and His eyes like a flame of fire; His feet were like fine brass, as if refined in a furnace, and His voice as the sound of many waters;" Revelation 1:13-15 (NKJV)

The image of God

People have been in arguments about what Jesus looked like. Every group, race, denomination have their opinion or picture of "the image of God" made flesh. Some have taken the location of where He was born, the race of His mother, and their image to create a picture. Few focus on "the image of God". Sounds familiar? Does it even matter about how He looked? I would say no due to the lack of details of His physical image. I found more on who He was, his actions, and his heart. He is the Son of God, the Word of God made flesh born without sin. This truth is what made looking into improving the beauty within important in the battle for more.

"Though he was God, he did not think of equality with God as something to cling to. Instead, he gave up his divine privileges; he took the humble posit of a slave and was born as a human being. When he appeared in human form, he humbled himself in obedience to God and died a criminal's death on a cross." Philippians 2:6-8 (NLT)

He was and still is above all else love, peace and grace. If you truly know Him, why is the physical image so important? Why is our physical image so important? To be in "the image of God" is about loving people where they are, for who they are. Who cares of their physical appearance? What is the appearance of their heart? To make the inner man in the most important, real "image of God" starts true transformation to the outer you.

The transformation of my image began with the knowledge and understanding of this. It was at this point that I focused less on the opinion others had about my physical image. Instead, I turned my focus on becoming more like "the image of God" that many spoke about and that I had begun reading about. I wanted more than anything to love me. The 'me' that God had created.

7 LOVING MORE

Love. What a powerful four-letter word that is used so freely, yet missing the true meaning behind it. Love is a profoundly, tender, passionate affection for another person per the definition. The word love is used mostly when speaking of family or our significant other. It is expected of us to say we love them, but there are limits to this love even with family. You do what I want or think I need, and I will love you. Do wrong to me, and I will love no more. Interesting enough, we are the same with ourselves. We love "self" if everything looks right or going as planned. Our love is conditional based on actions and feelings. Do we even understand what love is?

"...So, no matter what I say, what I believe, and what I do, I'm bankrupt without love. Love never gives up. Love cares more for others than for self. Love doesn't want what it doesn't have. Love doesn't strut, doesn't have a swelled head, doesn't force it self on others, isn't always "me first," doesn't fly off the handle, doesn't keep score of the sins of others, doesn't revel when others grovel, takes pleasure in the flowering of truth, puts up with anything, trusts God always, always looks for the best, never looks back, but keeps going to the end." 1 Corinthians 13:3-7 (MSG)

Learning to love more

It's no wonder we fall in and out of love with God. Though we may speak different, we place Him on the same level as any other person. In listening to others, our perception of God is vengeful. He will strike you where you stand for your sins or by our request. He will love you today and hate you instantly tomorrow if you do wrong. Sounds familiar? As stated before, it all begins with God. He has always loved us. We should spend time in knowing God and building a relationship with Him to find who He really is. It's through this relationship the process to love ourselves and others begin.

"For I was born a sinner-yes, from the moment my mother conceived me. But you desire honesty from the womb, teaching me wisdom even there." Psalms 51:5-6 (NLT)

Looking back, I can say that I've always sought ways to attempt death whether physically or mentally. Depression was real especially during my early years of high school. I was naturally quiet, so it caused no alarm when I sat in the classroom crying with my head down on the desk. Silence concealed my pain for many years from all the adults and even peers. I became very good at camouflaging the thoughts running through my head though silencing them was a different story. Smiling on que for the public eye in the day and crying myself to sleep at night. From the outside, everything looked perfect.

> *"All it takes is a beautiful fake smile to hide an injured soul, and they will never notice how broken you really are."*
> *Robin Williams*

Our parents and other adults around went through some similar if not the same situations that are experienced in our adolescent and young adult years. Unfortunately, they rarely share their truth. And as young people, we fail to share ours. It helps when a parent opens up about some parts of their life. I have found if we go to the beginning we may locate where it all began.

"Train up a child in the way he should go, and when he is old he will not depart from it." Proverbs 22:6 (NKJV)

I was in my late thirties when it happened to me. And when the door of opportunity opened, I asked one of my parents a few questions. It began with some basic questions like why did you get married. Eventually leading to a little more personal questions about decisions made and the effect they may have had on all involved. I suppose my line of questioning and conversation, though surprised, went well since I was asked later if I had ever wanted to be a psychiatrist or counselor.

By having this one conversation, my eyes were opened to see that there was a connection in my siblings' and my journey of despair. Each running from life in our own way. Some patterns of the past were showing up in the next generation. After some further conversations, I noticed various patterns have been going on for generations before and breaking out through the family tree. The passing along of unhealed pain, anger, broken hearts, and unhappiness. What a cycle to pass to each generation?

"My beloved friends, let us continue to love each other since love comes from God. Everyone who loves is born of God and experiences a relationship with God. The person who refuses to love doesn't know the first thing about God, because God is love – so you can't know him if you don't love. This is how God showed his love for us: God sent his only Son into the world so we might live through him. This is the kind of love we are talking about – not that we once upon a time loved God, but that he loved us and sent his Son as a sacrifice to clear away our sins and the damaged they've done to our relationship with God." 1 John 4:7-10 (MSG)

---

8 LEARNING TO FORGIVE MORE

After completing the chapter about love, I was unsure as to where to go next or did I need to add more to love. I took a breath, asked God what's next, and a small inner voice said forgive. I thought love was a little trying until I came across forgive. Even with love, forgiveness is sometimes hard to give. To forgive is to give up resentment of or to stop feeling anger toward someone. It sounds like I should have started with forgiveness before covering love, right? Well, I had to start with love first because God is love. It might have been hard to give or accept forgiveness if we didn't first cover and understand love. Few of us had a solid foundation of real love. We were missing the relationship with God and an understanding of His love. Forgiveness is hard with God, but even harder without Him.

Forgiveness

We all have someone in our life that we need to forgive. When we think forgive, I believe we look at it as giving a pass to the person that wronged us or caused pain. But the aforementioned is not about them. It's about you and your relationship with God. We are not responsible for what someone has done against us. We are responsible for our reaction to them and what was done. Yes, what they did was wrong, but you can't keep holding on to the hurt. Holding the pain of the past keeps you stuck in that place and prevents you from soaring to the next level, your purpose. You must forgive and release the burden of the pain to God. He can and will give you the freedom that you are supposed to live in.

"Get rid of all bitterness, rage, anger, harsh words, and slander, as well as all types of evil behavior. Instead, be kind to each other, tenderhearted, forgiving one another, just as God through Christ has forgiven you." Ephesians 4:31-32 (NLT)

I didn't understand this concept. I walked around for even some of my adult life holding on to some of the pains of my past. My actions were like the description above when I spoke of love except, I could barely say the word "love" to even family members, close or distant. A hug and kiss on the cheek which was hard to do did not have any meaning just an act that should happen when you see family.

Traveling this road to knowing God has taken damaged parts that were mended in my way and gracefully broke them to be healed by God. My patch work was not working. It limited me in so many areas from relationships to jobs to personal growth. I kept repeating the same cycle dressed in different clothes. I continued to get into relationships with the same types of people and settled for a bare minimum life. When I began yearning for a relationship with God, the band aid over my wounds began to be peeled off. Have you ever tried removing a band aid that has been on your skin for a while? You try to pull it very slow to prevent much pain. God did it the same for me and is still doing it.

Can I be a little vulnerable with you right now? My forgiveness needed to start at home. We had a lot that went on unknowingly to outsiders. I am the youngest of four, and being young, I did not understand some of the situations happening around me. Somewhere in my mind, I came up with the idea that some of it was my fault or maybe it would have been better if I was not there. With one unsuccessful attempt of suicide and a failed attempt to run away both around the age of five, I concluded that I was stuck, and stuck became a part of my cycle.

Here is where the work of forgiveness begins.

He will begin removing the items that patched the cracks of your foundation. Start by asking God to forgive you for all the things that you have done. I know what you are thinking, "I thought I was forgiven." Asking for forgiveness is about your acknowledgement of the wrong you've done, confession. Forgive yourself. One of the hardest parts in coming to know God is the awareness of your past. Before Him, you live your life on your terms, and you didn't care much about harming yourself. After Him, you are living your life for Him. Your actions become important to you. The blinders come off, and you not only realize but care about how much you did that was contrary to His Word. This awareness can bring great guilt and shame. Therefore, you have to remind yourself of His grace and the freedom given to you through Jesus Christ. This step may take a little while so don't get discouraged.

"Jesus prayed, "Father, forgive them; they don't know what they're doing." Luke 23:34 (MSG)

But there is more. Yes, He requires more. Remember those band aids. Now, God has you positioned to do and give more. Not because He demands it of you or make you feel guilty, you just want to be a better person for the One that loves you so much.

Forgive others. For example, the kids that bullied, picked fights, or told stories about you. Others may be the adult in the neighborhood that hurt you, or the one that falsely accused you of doing something wrong. Forgiving others can sometimes seem a little easier when you don't see them often, if at all, but God has a way of testing you. He will place you in a position where you would have to talk to them or better yet be the help they need. This may be difficult, but it will show the condition of your heart. Just when you get over that hurdle, He will expose another area. Sometimes, thoughts or a similar experience will remind you of the pain and who you once were which takes you back through steps of forgiving yourself.

The best example of forgiving others is Jesus. He had enemies before being born, and it didn't get any better as He got older. There was a time when He was discredited by people. It would have been an easy excuse to dislike or even hate them, but Jesus still forgave and asked God the Father to forgive them as well.

"But God, who through the preaching of all the prophets had said all along that his Messiah would be killed, knew exactly what you were doing and used it to fulfill his plans." Acts 3:18 (MSG)

But there is still more.

Forgive family.

Forgiving family can be the second hardest thing to do next to self. Your school and neighborhood can change by your choice, but you don't choose your family. You were born into your family. They were preselected. You may see them at reunions or when you go to your grandparents' house. When family hurt you, the pain runs deep.

These are the first people you encounter when born, and they are the first example of human love. Therefore, it may take some time to repair those cracks and may reopen some of the self-forgiveness cracks a little. When a parent chooses the streets over their family, it can make you question if you were ever important enough and their love. You may develop issues with your confidence and image when a sibling jokingly calls you a name based on your appearance. There are so many more issues that run deeper and cause great hurt.

In my journey of forgiving more, I had to ask God for help daily. I began to understand more that I needed to view the situations and the pain caused differently. I was not responsible for what others did or their why for doing it. I carried their weight of unforgiveness emotionally and physically along with my own. My conversations had to change along with my approach to them. Some people have the habit of unloading their emotional bags of garbage on you. When I stopped holding on to their baggage and viewpoint, it became a little easier to locate my own. I was able to throw out the bags of clutter that was preventing me from better relationships. Forgiving has its challenges, but it is possible to do by trusting the process and with time.

"Now we look inside, and what we see is that anyone united with the Messiah gets a fresh start, is created new. The old life is gone; a new life burgeons! Look at it! All this comes from the God who settled the relationship between us and him, and then called us to settle our relationships with each other. God put the world square with himself through the Messiah, giving the world a fresh start by offering forgiveness of sins. God has given us the task of telling everyone what he is doing. We're Christ's representatives. God uses us to persuade men and women to drop their differences and enter into God's work of making things right between them. We're speaking for Christ himself now: Become friends with God; he's already a friend with you." 2 Corinthians 5:17-20 (MSG)

9 TRUSTING MORE

I still have some struggles in this area with each new level of my life. Trust is confidence; surety of a person or thing. In life, we grow up trusting people that in some cases hurt us. Break us. Compromise our sense of existence.

There are so many people walking around with weakened foundations due to pains of the past. Parents abandoning kids to be raised by others. Fathers seeking other means of companionship outside of the home. Relatives abusing innocent children into their adolescence in some cases. Coworkers or people in authority spreading false accusations of others. Each instance damaging if not destroying the fabric of our trust. If I'm struggling to trust those I know and see daily, how do I trust someone that I have no proof of their existence? How do I trust the one that I blamed for my pain?

"Trust God from the bottom of your heart; don't try to figure out everything on your own. Listen for God's voice in everything you do, everywhere you go; he's the one who will keep you on track. Don't assume that you know it all. Run to God! Run from evil!" Proverbs 3:5-7 (MSG)

A battle with trusting more

In writing this, I've had to reflect on my own truths. My past. My present. My future. I had to face my own battle of trusting God. You see, I trust God to supply my need of food, shelter and clothing. I trust Him with the basic financial needs. My trust in God comes from what I've seen in my life. I have experienced some basic things that I know had to be Him because there was no other explanation. There have been times that I knew all my money wasn't going to cover the bills for the month or something I wanted, but it did. This may seem small in comparison, but that was the extent of my trust.

What about the big dreams that scare us to think about? What about the huge sacrifices that may need to happen for the vision He has placed inside of you? I've struggled. No, I am struggling to trust God with my whole heart. Can I see the vision? Yes. Do I believe it's going to happen?

Yes. Yet, I still have questions and doubts like when, are you sure, and the world famous...how.

Big things...big trust and definitely faith.

"Why are you so polite with me, always saying 'Yes, sir', and 'That's right, sir', but never doing a thing I tell you? These words I speak to you are not mere additions to your life, homeowner improvements to your standard of living. They are foundation words, words to build a life on." Luke 6:46-47 (MSG)

Trusting God is difficult for several reasons. One, we don't really know Him. By knowing, I am referring to a relationship which is why I felt that needed to be covered in the beginning. Two, we must relinquish our control to Him.

Most of our life, we have a plan for the where, who with, and how it's done. Plans are good because they help keep you focused. But once you see a glimpse of His plans, get ready. There is no way you can control or direct His plans. Your attempt in controlling it is like a baby pushing its stroller when they first learn to walk. It looks like they have it under control until they run into everything in their path. You can tell them to go in a direction, but they still do what they want.

Like us, they are unable to see what's in front of them. Like us, they get mad when you try to help them because they have a plan. Just like us, they don't realize it's easier with your help until they release their control. The baby doesn't know when you need them to turn because you haven't told them. They are not positioned to see the obstacles ahead. And no matter how much they want to prove to you that they can do it, they still require the guidance that only you can provide.

Trust

That is what it's like to trust God. We will need to relinquish our need to control to Him. There will be obstacles ahead that only He can guide us through. For if we knew about them, we wouldn't proceed. Then, if He revealed the entire plan, we would try to do it without Him. He knows we can handle it, but He wants to be a part of it. He created us for the purpose of doing His will on earth.

In trusting God with your whole heart, you can no longer just go through the motions of life based on your agenda. It's not easy, and He will take you through some test runs. The thing is knowing His voice, do what He says do and when He says do it.

"If we claim that we're free of sin, we're only fooling ourselves. A claim like that is errant nonsense. On the other hand, if we admit our sins-make a clean breast of them-he won't let us down; he'll be true to himself. He'll forgive our sins and purge us of all wrongdoing. If we claim that we've never sinned, we out-and -out contradict God-make a liar out of him. A claim like that only shows off our ignorance of God." 1 John 1:8-10 (MSG)

I am worth more!

Could my worth be another hindrance in my trust in God?

Worth is the value of something measured by its qualities or by the esteem in which it is held; moral or personal value. If I'm honest with myself, there are times that I have questioned if I'm worthy to have or even ask for the big things. I have found myself attempting to include people in my dreams for this very reason. I suppose that I have never really felt deserving of more, so I have always played the background of the dreams of other people. Now don't misunderstand me. I have totally enjoyed every moment of helping others in every way, and I can see now how it has prepared me for this season. Some saw my help as me being used by the other person or thought I should receive monetary compensation for my work. I didn't see it that way. Reflecting back, I was given opportunity after opportunity to be a part of and see God work in ways that I couldn't imagine. I was learning how to trust God through others and to witness what having faith really look like. And trust me when I say, it did not look as I had perceived.

Why do I not feel worthy or trust God for the big things now?

I have always looked for my worth from people especially those that I trusted or thought I was able to. Also, from my perception at one time, I was not important enough. Now, I'm faced with a journey that I have never taken alone or led. I am facing the obstacles that I've witnessed with no one to hide behind.

I am learning how to lead from the front when I have never seen myself as a front row person. Learning that God took me through those experiences for a time such as this. Learning I am worthy of more regardless of my past because of God and His love for me. Realizing, I am important enough, and it has nothing to do with people. Knowing now, I can only sustain this by putting Him first in everything and talking to Him about all things.

10 PRAYING MORE

One thing about everything written to this point, you will revisit in different seasons of your life. It's called growth. I can't begin to tell you how many times that I came back to love and forgiveness. How many times my relationship and knowing God has changed with each situation that I have faced in life. How many times I had to be reminded to trust God which reflected to my relationship with Him.

"One day he was praying in a certain place. When he finished, one of his disciples said, "Master, teach us to pray just as John taught his disciples." Luke 11:1 (MSG)

Currently, I am learning more about prayer. Our relationship with God has a lot to do with prayer as well. Prayer is defined as a spiritual communion with God;

talking to God. For years, I have done this one-way conversation with God not even for sure He was on the other end. I went through the actions of the proper posture as seen in my past. My conversation consisted of me briefly telling selected information and the occasional thank you for the "real" good things that happened.

Are you like me?

I compartmentalized the things that I prayed about. If something "major" happened, I thanked Him. If something I didn't see myself being able to handle, I asked for help. If someone made me mad enough, I asked Him to do something with them. There were parts of my life that I took for granted and didn't thank Him for. I tried to handle even the smallest of issues myself in my way. And for those that upset me, they had the issue and forgiveness almost unseen.

"Don't fret or worry. Instead of worrying, pray. Let petitions and praises shape your worries into prayers, letting God know your concerns. Before you know it, a sense of God's wholeness, everything coming together for good, will come and settle you down. It's wonderful what happens when Christ displaces worry at the center of your life." Philippians 4:6-7 (MSG)

These days, I spend most mornings sipping a cup of coffee, reading a devotional and God's Word. Then, I sit quietly in wait for the words to write in my journal. I like to think of each page as my letter to God and a way to release those thoughts that used to keep me on an emotional rollercoaster. Also, I listen for what He wants to say to me because I've learned He is definitely talking. These moments have been the best for me. It sets a positive tone for my day. I still struggle at times with this. There are occasions that I haven't brought something to Him in prayer whether in my writing or in my quiet time. Just when I begin to worry or feel stressed, I'm reminded "I didn't take this to Him".

Looking back on that day of hearing the words "Let go", I know now it wasn't all about the relationship as I thought. I have faced many obstacles in my past. The pain had left many open unhealed wounds. I was hiding, feeling shame for the decisions that I made or didn't make. In my mind, there was an image that I had to live up to. And, I had missed the mark, in my opinion, causing additional shame to my family as well as myself.

I have come to understand the obstacles. Each one was used to draw me closer to God and teach me more of the person He created me to be. God was and is teaching me what it means to really trust Him. It gets hard at times, and the obstacles haven't stopped just as my journey hasn't. I'm establishing a relationship with Him. And like most relationships, you go through, talk through and grow through.

Letting go.

Letting go was about all the things that were holding me back from the relationship that I needed most. It was about letting go of the guilt and shame from my past. Forgiving myself and others that hurt me whether directly or indirectly. It was about letting go of trying to live up to the expectations of people. And, letting go of the fear. Fear of failing at anything that I attempt and fear of succeeding because I didn't think that I was worthy to have it. It was about letting go and filling every space with God's love and grace.

I'm still letting go and learning to depend on God in all areas. I'm learning to let go of the 'I' for the 'Him'. I'm learning to talk and even more so listen. I'm learning to focus less on the problems and my frustrations to them. Instead, I place my focus on God. I am asking what He wants me to do. I am asking what am I supposed to learn from this. Don't get me wrong. It sounds like I have it all worked out, but I still have my moments as we all do. I still struggle occasionally with obeying Him, hearing Him and I still question some things. There are times, I question if I'm really the person chosen to speak up, write, and help. They are getting better with each day (in my opinion of course), and then He reveals something else.

Lessons.

Not that I understand why things had to happen as they did, I do understand that God has a reason for all we go through. Keywords "go through". If I had stopped going through that relationship mentioned earlier, I may have settled for what people wanted for me instead of seeking more. The battles in that relationship from the outside was designed to take me out, but God had a plan. The one being used to take me out ended up being the one to encourage me to see more. And with that, the battle pushed a little girl onto the path of becoming what she didn't believe to be possible for her. If I had stopped going through and never started the journey, you wouldn't be reading this book, and I wouldn't have been able to encourage the many people that have crossed my path prior to.

I think back occasionally and cry for the little girl that I once was. Not because I feel sorry for her, I cry tears of joy for her fight, her seeking, who she has become and who she is becoming.

With all she experienced those mentioned and most unmentioned, she survived. She survived the repeated attempts of silencing the pain. She survived the attacks of who people said she was. She survived the feeling of abandonment during key moments in her life. She survived the things that were meant to take her out. And you will too! The courage in sharing a part of my story is to offer encouragement to whomever reads this. I want you to know that we are all on a journey and none is perfect. Like most roads we travel, there will be bumps, potholes and detours, but keep going. Don't allow stopping to be an option because if you stop all those behind you will too.

In this season, I read God's Word more. Seek understanding and ask questions along with learning to study. I listen for His voice and write in my journal often. In doing this, I have found a greater want to love Him and to love me. There are things that I do now because of Him that was hard before. With each day, I want to learn to genuinely love people. I want to know Him even more, and it's not because someone said to do it. I want to get out of the way and allow Him to continue the transformation in me.

Sometimes, I blindly jump in the midst of my fear because now I know more than ever that He's got me. And, it reminds me every time that "I can do all things through God who strengthens me." (Phil 4:13)

A Battle For More

ABOUT THE AUTHOR

Chanda Ford is a native of Northeast Louisiana. She has worked professionally in local government for 19 years. Her work in local government has allowed her to meet and assist people from all walks of life. Over the years, her work has ignited a passion to help people of all ages which has led her to serving in numerous capacities such as a board member in education and ministry.

The journey that Chanda has embarked upon has led her to entrepreneurship as well. After talking about health to many people for years, she stopped fighting to be in the background and decided to become the Owner of IAMPHIT LLC. Chanda's business is allowing her the opportunity to help people love themselves, to have a different perspective on life's situations and to live their best life in the season they are in.

www.ingramcontent.com/pod-product-compliance
Lightning Source LLC
Chambersburg PA
CBHW031526040426
42445CB00009B/422